CW00742041

Burgers & Smoothies

TARLA DALAL
■ INDIA'S #1 COOKERY AUTHOR ■

S&C
SANJAY & CO.
MUMBAI

COOKBOOKS BY TARLA DALAL

INDIAN COOKING
Tava Cooking
Rotis & Subzis
Desi Khana
The Complete Gujarati Cook Book
Mithai
Chaat
Achaar aur Parathe
The Rajasthani Cookbook
Swadisht Subzian
Punjabi Khana
Mughlai Khana
South Indian Recipes

TOTAL HEALTH
Low Calorie Healthy Cooking
Pregnancy Cookbook
Baby and Toddler Cookbook
Cooking with 1 Teaspoon of Oil
Home Remedies
Delicious Diabetic Recipes
Fast Foods Made Healthy
Healthy Soups & Salads
Healthy Breakfast
Calcium Rich Recipes
Healthy Heart Cook Book
Forever Young Diet
Healthy Snacks
Iron Rich Recipes
Healthy Juices
Low Cholesterol Recipes
Good Food for Diabetes
Healthy Subzis
Healthy Snacks for Kids

High Blood Pressure Cook Book
Low Calorie Sweets
Nutritious Recipes for Pregnancy
Diabetic Snacks
Zero Oil Rotis & Subzis
Zero Oil Soups, Salads & Snacks
Zero Oil Dal & Chawal
Acidity Cook Book
Growing Kids Cookbook
Soya Rotis & Subzis
Cooking with Sprouts
Exotic Diabetic Cooking - Part 1
Healthy Diabetic Cooking
Protein Rich Recipes
Eat Well Stay Well
Weight Loss after Pregnancy
100 Calorie Snacks
Top 10 Healthy Foods [New]
Healthy Starters [New]

WESTERN COOKING
The Complete Italian Cookbook
The Chocolate Cookbook
Eggless Desserts
Mocktails & Snacks
Thai Cooking
Soups & Salads
Mexican Cooking
Chinese Cooking
Easy Chinese Cooking
Sizzlers & Barbeques
Cakes & Pastries
Party Drinks
Wraps & Rolls
Mousses, Cheesecakes & Cupcakes [New]
Burgers & Smoothies [New]

MINI SERIES
Cooking Under 10 minutes
Pizzas and Pasta
Fun Food for Children
Roz ka Khana
Idlis & Dosas
Microwave Desi Khana
Paneer
Parathas
Chawal
Dals
Sandwiches
Quick Cooking
Curries & Kadhis
Chinese Recipes
Jain Desi Khana
7 Dinner Menus
Jain International Recipes
Punjabi Subzis
Chips & Dips

Corn
Microwave Subzis
Baked Dishes
Stir-Fry
Potatoes
Recipes Using Leftovers
Noodles
Lebenese
Cook Book for Two's
Know your Dals & Pulses
Fruit & Vegetable Carving
Know your Spices
Know your Flours
Popular Restaurant Gravies
Know Your Green Leafy Vegetables
Paneer Snacks
Pressure Cooker Recipes
Faraal Foods for Fasting Days
Finger Foods for Kids
Microwave Desi Khana - Part II

GENERAL COOKING
Exciting Vegetarian Cooking
Microwave Recipes
Saatvik Khana
The Pleasures of Vegetarian Cooking
The Delights of Vegetarian Cooking
The Joys of Vegetarian Cooking
Cooking with Kids
Snacks Under 10 Minutes
Ice-Cream & Frozen Desserts
Desserts Under 10 Minutes
Entertaining
Microwave Snacks & Desserts
Kebabs & Tikkis
Non-fried Snacks
Mumbai's Roadside Snacks
Tiffin Treats for Kids

First Printing : 2012

Copyright © Sanjay & Co.

ISBN : 978-93-80392-16-5

Price Rs. 299/-

Published & Distributed by :
SANJAY & COMPANY
353/A-1, Shah & Nahar Industrial Estate, Dhanraj Mill Compound, Lower Parel (W), Mumbai - 400 013. INDIA.
Tel. : (91-22) 4345 2400 • Fax : (91-22) 2496 5876

"Tarla Dalal" is also a registered trademark owned by Sanjay & Co.
ALL RIGHTS RESERVED WITH THE PUBLISHERS.
No portion of this book shall be reproduced, stored in retrieval system or transmitted by any means, electronic, mechanical, photocopying, recording or otherwise, without the written permission of the publishers.

Disclaimer : While every precaution has been taken in the preparation of this book, the publishers and the author assume no responsibility for errors or omissions. Neither is any liability assumed for damages resulting from the use of information contained herein.

Bulk Purchases : Tarla Dalal Cookbooks are ideal gifts. If you are interested in buying more than 500 assorted copies of Tarla Dalal Cookbooks at special prices, please contact us at 91-22-4345 2400 or email : sanjay@tarladalal.com

For books, Membership on **tarladalal.com,** Subscription for **Cooking & More** and Recipe queries
Timing : 9.30 a.m. to 6.00 p.m., Monday to Friday, 9.30 a.m. to 1.00 p.m. Saturday
Contact : Tel. : (91-22) 4345 2400 • Fax : (91-22) 2496 5876
E-mail : ravindra@tarladalal.com • sanjay@tarladalal.com

Recipe Research
Nisha Katira
Payal Shah
Neha Mirlekar

Photography
Sanjay Dalal

Food Stylist
Nisha Katira

Assistant Food Stylist
Payal Shah
Neha Mirlekar

Design
Satyamangal Rege

Copy Editor
Janani Gopalkrishnan Vikram

Typesetting
Adityas Enterprises

Printed by
Minal Sales Agencies

Dear friends,

've always considered burgers as much more than mere snacks. With a wholesome bun, tasty cutlet, cheese and lots of salad veggies, it is actually a very sumptuous meal. Add a glass of nutritious and tasty smoothie to a filling burger, and voila, you actually have a meal out there—whether for kids or adults. What I like very much about both burgers and smoothies is that you can put your intelligence and imagination to good use and come up with a lot of interesting combinations. And although a burger actually appears to involve too many preparations, it can finally be put together in a jiffy before serving. In all, a very interesting combination, and so I think you will also like this new book on **'Burgers and Smoothies'**.

The first section has recipes for 12 **burgers**. People think burgers can have only a vegetable cutlet, but in this book I have explored a lot more options like **Hara Tava Burger, page 8, Falafel Burger, page 22,** etc. I have also stayed away from plain mayonnaise and tried more interesting variants like chilli mayonnaise in the **Veggie Burger, page 10,** and parsley mayonnaise in the **Brocooli Burger, page 20**. In some recipes, I have totally skipped the mayonnaise and substituted it with salsa as in the recipe of the Three Bean Burger, page 18, and spring onion spread as has been used in the **Rajma Burger, page 12.** There is a suggestion for health freaks too—you can avoid deep-frying the cutlet and instead opt for shallow-frying.

French fries is one thing that goes hand-in-hand with burgers… it makes your mouth drool and yearn for more. Learn how to make perfect French fries in the second section on **Accompaniments**. Apart from that, explore a few more varieties of French fries like **Chilli Garlic Fries, page 37,** and **Masala French Fries, page 42**. Some other crunchy accompaniments like **Fried Mozzarella Sticks, page 36, Khimchi, page 43,** and **Cheesy Potato Chips, page 38,** also feature in this section, which comprises of 12 recipes totally.

The third section on **Smoothies** includes 24 recipes, made with a variety of fruits and fruit juices combined with curds and/or ice-cream. These smoothies are sure to quench your thirst and round off your meal quite aptly! Once you try the burger-smoothie combination, you will not even dream of ordering an aerated drink with your meal next time. **Apple Smoothie, page 69, Melon Smoothie, page 56,** and **Mango Banana Smoothie,** page 58, hit the list of common smoothies, while **Flax Seeds Smoothie, page 52, Thai Smoothie, page 53,** and **Anjeer Smoothie, page 63,** are amongst the innovative new ones. While burgers take a toll on time, the smoothies can be whipped up in a jiffy.

Each section has a few pointers to follow to make these recipes a perfect hit. I suggest you read and follow them. Go ahead and try these recipes with confidence… they are easy and fun-filled. Plus, as I mentioned right in the beginning, it's all about innovation—think freely, make your own combinations of burger, accompaniment and smoothie and rock the party!
Regards

Burgers.....6

CONTENTS

Accompaniments 32

Smoothies.....46

Top 10 Tips
to assemble
a burger

1 Toasting the burger bun halves lightly is very important to make the buns softer.

2 Always chop the vegetables for the cutlet very finely.

3 Do not mash or mix the cutlet mixture too much or else it will be difficult to shape them into round.

4 If the cutlet is not firm enough add a little cornflour or bread crumbs.

5 Dip the cutlet well in the plain flour mixture and bread crumbs to avoid it from disintegrating while deep-frying and also to get a crispy texture.

Burger

6. To save on calories, shallow fry the cutlets with minimum oil rather than deep-frying.
7. You can make the cutlet mixture and spreads in advance but deep-fry the cutlet and assemble the burger just before serving else it will turn soggy.
8. Spreads made in advance and vegetables like tomato, cucumber and lettuce cut in advance are best refrigerated till use.
9. The best lettuce variety to be used for burgers is Iceberg followed by Roman.
10. If you like melted cheese in the burger, assemble the burger, put it in a microwave-safe plate and microwave on HIGH for 20 seconds. Serve immediately.

Hara Tava Burger

There are many exciting aspects to the Hara Tava Burger! Most notably, there is the unique cutlet made up of green chick peas and spinach, which explains the name of this burger! Then, there is a zesty side that adults will love, all thanks to the spicy mayonnaise and the cheesy, herby potato wedges. I would like to draw your attention to the bread slices used in this recipe and in many others… they play a very important role, acting as a binding agent and also ensuring that the cutlet is soft.

PREPARATION TIME: 20 MINUTES.
COOKING TIME: 15 TO 20 MINUTES.
MAKES 4 BURGERS.

For the *cutlets*
2 cups soaked and cooked *hara chana* (green chick peas)
1½ tsp oil
¼ cup roughly chopped onions
1½ tbsp roughly chopped green chillies
1 tbsp roughly chopped garlic (*lehsun*)
1¼ cups roughly chopped spinach (*palak*)
½ tsp chilli powder
Salt and freshly ground black pepper powder to taste
2 bread slices, crumbled
½ cup plain flour (*maida*) dissolved in ¾ cup water
Bread crumbs for rolling
Oil for deep-frying

To be mixed together for spicy mayonnaise spread
½ cup eggless mayonnaise
2 tbsp red chilli sauce
½ tsp mustard sauce

Other ingredients
4 burger buns
4 tsp melted butter
4 lettuce leaves
4 cheese slices
12 cucumber slices
8 tomato slices
4 onion slices
Salt and freshly ground pepper to taste

Accompaniments
Spicy Cheese and Herb Potato Wedges, page 34

For the *cutlets*
1. Heat the oil in a non-stick pan, add the onions, green chillies and garlic and sauté on a medium flame for 2 to 3 minutes.
2. Add the spinach, mix well and cook on a medium flame for 2 to 3 minutes, while stirring once in between.
3. Add the cooked *hara chana*, chilli powder, salt and pepper powder and sauté on a medium flame for another 2 to 3 minutes. Keep aside to cool slightly.
4. Add the bread slices and 2 tbsp of water and blend in a mixer to a coarse paste.
5. Transfer the mixture into a bowl, divide it into 4 equal portions and shape each portion into a circle of 75 mm. (3") diameter and 1 cm thickness.
6. Dip each *cutlet* in the plain flour mixture and roll in the bread crumbs till it is evenly coated from all the sides.
7. Heat the oil in a *kadhai* and deep-fry each *cutlet* till it turns golden brown in colour from both the sides. Drain on absorbent paper and keep aside.

How to proceed
1. Cut each burger bun horizontally into two. Apply ½ tsp of butter on the insides of each half of the burger bun and toast them lightly on a *tava* (griddle). Keep aside.
2. Place a lower half of the bun on a clean, dry surface with the buttered side facing up.
3. Place 1 lettuce leaf and apply 2 tbsp of the spicy mayonnaise spread evenly over it.
4. Place a *cutlet*, 1 cheese slice, 3 cucumber slices, 2 tomato slices and 1 onion slice and sprinkle a little salt and pepper over it.
5. Cover with an upper half of a bun with the buttered side facing down and press it lightly.
6. Repeat with the remaining ingredients to make 3 more burgers.
   Serve immediately with Spicy Cheese and Herb Potato Wedges.

Veggie Burger

PREPARATION TIME: 30 MINUTES.
COOKING TIME: 30 TO 35 MINUTES.
MAKES 4 BURGERS.

*T*he Veggie Burger is one of the most common burgers around, but let me tell you upfront that this recipe is not a run-of-the-mill one! It is a wonderful indo-western combo, as the tikki imbibes true Indian spices while the spread uses chilli sauce and oregano to perk up the mayonnaise. Also, unlike the common burgers in which the vegetables are boiled, here we use raw vegetables sautéed to perfection. The complementary colours of the capsicum and potatoes in the salad ensure that it looks very tempting too!

For the *cutlets*
½ cup finely chopped onions
1 cup finely chopped potatoes
½ cup finely chopped French beans
½ cup finely chopped carrots
½ cup finely chopped cabbage
2 tbsp oil
1 tsp chilli powder
¼ tsp turmeric powder (*haldi*)
Salt to taste
¼ cup plain flour (*maida*)
2 tbsp finely chopped coriander (*dhania*)
½ cup plain flour (*maida*) dissolved in ¾ cup water
Bread crumbs for rolling
Oil for deep-frying

For the chilli mayo spread
2 tbsp chilli sauce
4 tbsp mayonnaise
1 tsp finely chopped garlic (*lehsun*)
1 tsp oregano

For the salad
1 cup sliced coloured capsicum (red, yellow and green)
½ cup boiled and peeled potatoes, cut into long strips like French fries
1 tbsp butter
Salt and freshly ground pepper powder to taste

Other ingredients
4 burger buns
4 tsp melted butter
4 lettuce leaves
4 cheese slices

Accompaniments
French Fries, page 35

For the *cutlets*
1. Heat the oil in a deep non-stick, add the onions and sauté on a medium flame for a minute.
2. Add all the vegetables, cover with a lid and cook on a medium flame for 10 minutes or till the vegetables are cooked, while stirring occasionally. Sprinkle a little water to avoid the vegetables from burning.
3. Add the chilli powder, turmeric powder and salt and sauté on a medium flame for a minute.
4. Add the plain flour and cook on a medium flame for 2 minutes, while stirring continuously.
5. Remove from the flame, add the coriander and mix well.
6. While the mixture is yet hot, mash it using a potato masher to a coarse mixture.
7. Divide it into 4 equal portions and shape each portion into a circle of 75 mm. (3") diameter and 1 cm thickness.
8. Dip each *cutlet* in the plain flour mixture and roll in the bread crumbs till it is evenly coated from all the sides.
9. Heat the oil in a *kadhai* and deep-fry each *cutlet* till it turns golden brown in colour from both the sides. Drain on absorbent paper and keep aside.

For the chilli mayo spread
1. Combine all the ingredients in a deep bowl and mix well.
2. Divide the spread into 2 equal portions and keep aside.

For the salad
1. Heat the butter in a broad non-stick pan, add the coloured capsicum and sauté on a medium flame for 2 to 3 minutes.
2. Add the salt and pepper and sauté on a medium flame for a minute.
3. Add the potatoes and sauté on a medium flame for another minute.
4. Remove from the flame and keep aside to cool.

5. Add 1 portion of the chilli mayo spread and mix well.
6. Divide the salad into 4 equal portions and keep aside.

How to proceed
1. Cut each burger bun horizontally into two. Apply ½ tsp of butter on the insides of each half of the burger bun and toast them lightly on a *tava* (griddle). Keep aside.
2. Apply ¾ tbsp of the chilli mayo spread on the buttered side of all the burger bun halves.
3. Place the lower half of a bun on a clean, dry surface with the buttered–spread side facing up.
4. Place 1 lettuce leaf, a *cutlet* and 1 cheese slice over it.
5. Spread 1 portion of the salad over it, cover with an upper half of a bun with the buttered–spread side facing down and press it lightly.
6. Repeat with the remaining ingredients to make 3 more burgers.
   Serve immediately with French Fries.

Rajma Burger

*C*hoose the Rajma Burger when you want to ensure a unique menu for your party! With a rajma and paneer cutlet, and a unique curd-based spring onion spread that is very uncommon in burgers, this one is sure to impress your guests. Since this burger does not use cheese, serve it with Mozzarella Sticks, to complete the platter.

PREPARATION TIME: 30 MINUTES.
COOKING TIME: 20 TO 25 MINUTES.
MAKES 4 BURGERS.

For the *cutlets*
1 cup soaked, boiled and drained *rajma* (kidney beans)
1½ tsp oil
¾ cup sliced onions
1 tbsp finely chopped ginger (*adrak*)
1½ tsp finely chopped green chillies
½ tsp turmeric powder (*haldi*)
½ cup boiled, peeled and mashed potatoes
⅓ cup grated *paneer* (cottage cheese)
⅓ cup chopped coriander (*dhania*)
1 tsp *garam masala*
Salt to taste
2 tbsp cornflour
½ cup plain flour (*maida*) dissolved in ¾ cup water for rolling
Bread crumbs for rolling
Oil for deep-frying

For the spring onion spread
⅓ cup thick chilled curds (*dahi*)
¼ cup chopped spring onions (including the greens)
¼ tsp chopped garlic (*lehsun*)
¼ tsp chopped green chillies
A pinch cumin seeds (*jeera*) powder
¼ tsp sugar
¼ tsp mustard powder
Salt to taste

Other ingredients
1 tbsp oil
8 onion rings
4 capsicum rings
1 tbsp dry red chilli flakes
1 tbsp dried mixed herbs
Salt and freshly ground pepper to taste
4 burger buns
4 tsp melted butter
4 lettuce leaves

Accompaniments
Fried Mozzarella Sticks, page 36

For the *cutlets*
1. Mash the *rajma* coarsely and keep aside.
2. Heat the oil in a broad non-stick pan, add the onions, ginger and green chillies and sauté on a medium flame for 4 to 5 minutes.
3. Add the turmeric powder, potatoes, *paneer, rajma,* coriander, *garam masala* and salt, mix well and cook on a medium flame for 3 to 4 minutes, while stirring continuously.
4. Remove from the flame, cool slightly and add the cornflour and mix well.
5. Divide it into 4 equal portions and shape each portion into a circle of 75 mm. (3") diameter and 1 cm thickness.
6. Dip each *cutlet* in the plain flour mixture and roll in the bread crumbs till it is evenly coated from all the sides.
7. Heat the oil in a *kadhai* and deep-fry each *cutlet* till it turns golden brown in colour from both the sides. Drain on absorbent paper and keep aside.

For the spring onion spread
1. Combine all the ingredients along with 1 tbsp of curds and blend in a mixer to a smooth paste.
2. Transfer the paste into a bowl, add the remaining curds and mix well. Keep aside.

How to proceed
1. Heat the oil in a non-stick pan, add the onion and capsicum rings and sauté gently on a medium flame for 2 minutes.
2. Add the chilli flakes, mixed herbs, salt and pepper and sauté gently on a medium flame for another 30 seconds.
3. Remove from the flame and keep aside.
4. Cut each burger bun horizontally into two. Apply ½ tsp of butter on the insides of each half of the burger bun and toast them lightly on a *tava* (griddle). Keep aside.
5. Apply 1 tbsp of the spring onion spread on all the upper bun halves and keep aside.

6. Place the lower half of a bun on a clean, dry surface with the buttered side facing up.
7. Place 1 lettuce leaf and 1 onion ring and apply 1 tbsp of the spring onion spread over it.
8. Place a *cutlet*, 1 capsicum ring and 1 onion ring over it.
9. Place the upper half of a bun over it with the buttered-spread side facing down and press it lightly.
10. Repeat with the remaining ingredients to make 3 more burgers.
Serve immediately with Fried Mozzarella Sticks.

Hara Bhara Burger

*T*angy, spicy, tempting… name it and you'll get it in this super-duper Hara Bhara burger! The popular Hara Bhara Cutlet, usually served as a starter, is combined with marinated paneer and onion rings to make a delectable burger. Regular fries perked up with chilli powder and garlic makes a great accompaniment for this burger, while the green chutney adds a minty touch.

PREPARATION TIME: 25 MINUTES.
COOKING TIME: 30 MINUTES.
MAKES 4 BURGERS.
SOAKING TIME: 1 HOUR.

For the *cutlets*
¾ cup roughly chopped blanched and drained spinach (*palak*)
3 tbsp *chana dal* (split Bengal gram)
1½ tsp roughly chopped ginger (*adrak*)
1½ tsp roughly chopped garlic (*lehsun*)
1½ tbsp finely chopped green chillies
⅓ cup boiled green peas
⅓ cup grated *paneer* (cottage cheese)
⅓ cup boiled, peeled and mashed potatoes
¾ tsp *chaat masala*
½ tsp *garam masala*
¾ cup bread crumbs
Salt to taste
¼ cup plain flour dissolved with ⅓ cup of water
½ cup plain flour (*maida*) dissolved in ¾ cup water for rolling
Oil for deep-frying

For the green *chutney* (makes approx. 10 tbsp)
2 cups roughly chopped mint leaves (*phudina*)
1 cup roughly chopped coriander (*dhania*)
2 tsp cumin seeds (*jeera*)
2 tbsp roughly chopped green chillies
2 tsp lemon juice
Salt to taste
2 tbsp fresh cream

Other ingredients
½ cup mayonnaise
12 slices of *paneer* (cottage cheese), cut into 50 mm. (2") x 25 mm. (1") and 1 cm. thick
12 onion rings
2 tsp oil
4 burger buns
4 tsp melted butter
4 cheese slices

Accompaniments
Chilli Garlic Fries, page 37

For the *cutlets*
1. Clean, wash and soak the *chana dal* in a bowl for 1 hour. Drain well.
2. Add the ginger, garlic, green chillies and ¾ cup of water and pressure cook for 3 whistles or until the *dal* is cooked. Drain and discard any excess water. Cool slightly and keep aside.
3. Combine the spinach, green peas and cooked *dal* mixture and blend in a mixer to a coarse paste without using any water.
4. Transfer the paste into a bowl, add the *paneer*, potatoes, *chaat masala*, *garam masala*, half the bread crumbs and salt and mix well.
5. Divide it into 4 equal portions and shape each portion into a circle of 75 mm. (3") diameter and 1 cm thickness.
6. Dip each *cutlet* in the plain flour mixture and roll in the remaining bread crumbs till it is evenly coated from all the sides.
7. Heat the oil in a *kadhai* and deep-fry each *cutlet* till it turns golden brown in colour from both the sides. Drain on absorbent paper and keep aside.

For the green *chutney*
1. Combine all the ingredients, except the cream and blend in a mixer to a smooth paste.
2. Transfer it into a bowl, add the cream and mix well. Keep aside.

How to proceed
1. Combine the mayonnaise and 5 tbsp of the green *chutney* in a deep bowl and mix well. Keep the green mayonnaise aside.
2. Combine the *paneer* slices, onion rings and the remaining 5 tbsp of the green *chutney* in another bowl and toss gently. Keep aside to marinate for 15 minutes.
3. Heat the oil in a non-stick pan, add the marinated *paneer* and onions and sauté gently on a medium flame for 5 minutes or till the

paneer pieces turn light brown in colour from all the sides. Keep aside.

4. Cut each burger bun horizontally into two. Apply ½ tsp of butter on the insides of each half of the burger bun and toast them lightly on a *tava* (griddle).

5. Apply 1 tbsp of the green mayonnaise on buttered side of all the bun halves.

6. Place the lower half of a bun on a clean, dry surface with the buttered–green mayonnaise side facing up.

7. Place a *cutlet* and 1 cheese slice over it.

8. Again apply 1 tbsp of the green mayonnaise, place 3 sautéed *paneer* slices and 3 sautéed onion rings and cover with an upper half of a bun with the buttered–green mayonnaise side facing down and press it lightly.

9. Repeat with the remaining ingredients to make 3 more burgers.
Serve immediately with Chilli Garlic Fries.

Spinach and Corn Open Burger

*Y*ou would surely have tried open sandwiches. What about an exceptional open burger? Try this different recipe, and you are sure to fall in love with it. Instead of a cutlet, the Spinach and Corn Open Burger uses a rich filling of spinach and corn combined with cream and mozzarella cheese. The cheesy potato chips served as an accompaniment with this burger makes it all the more attractive.

PREPARATION TIME: 20 MINUTES.
COOKING TIME: 10 TO 12 MINUTES.
MAKES 8 OPEN BURGERS.

For the filling
1 cup blanched and chopped spinach (*palak*)
1 cup boiled sweet corn kernels (*makai ke dane*)
1 tbsp butter
¼ cup finely chopped onions
1 tsp finely chopped green chillies
Salt and freshly ground pepper to taste
1 tbsp cornflour dissolved in ¼ cup chilled milk
1 tbsp fresh cream
2 tbsp grated mozzarella cheese

Other ingredients
4 burger buns
4 tsp melted butter
16 tomato slices
8 cucumber slices
16 onion slices
12 tbsp grated cheese
1 tbsp dry red chilli flakes

Accompaniments
Cheesy Potato Chips, page 38

For the filling
1. Heat the butter in a broad non-stick pan, add the onions and green chillies and sauté on a medium flame for a minute.
2. Add the spinach, corn, salt and pepper, mix well and sauté on a medium flame for another 2 minutes.
3. Add the cornflour-milk paste, mix well and cook on a medium flame for 2 minutes or till the mixture becomes thick.
4. Add the fresh cream, mix well and cook on a medium flame for 1 more minute.
5. Remove from the flame, add the cheese and mix well. Keep aside.

How to proceed
1. Cut each burger bun horizontally into two and scoop out the centres of each bun half so as to form a little depression.
2. Butter each burger bun half using ½ tsp of butter and toast them lightly on a *tava* (griddle).
3. Place the bun halves on a clean, dry surface with the inner side facing up.
4. Fill each scooped bun half with 2 tbsp of the filling and place 2 tomato slices, 1 cucumber slice and 2 onion slices over it.
5. Sprinkle 1½ tbsp of cheese and a little chilli flakes over it.
6. Place 2 such open burgers on a microwave safe plate and microwave on HIGH for 20 seconds.
7. Repeat the step 6 to make 6 more open burgers in 3 more batches.
   Serve immediately with Cheesy Potato Chips.

Three Bean Burger

As the name Three Bean Burger suggests, this high-protein delight combines three tasty beans – rajma, chawli and kabuli chana – with vegetables. Paneer and bread crumbs act as binding agents, while the uncooked salsa imparts a Mexican touch. No fuss, easily made, but you just need to remember to make the curd spread in advance as the curds have to be hung for half an hour. This will help to remove any excess water and give a thick spread – after all, nobody likes a soggy burger!

PREPARATION TIME: 30 MINUTES.
COOKING TIME: 20 TO 25 MINUTES.
MAKES 4 BURGERS.

For the *cutlets*
1 cup mixed beans (*rajma, chawli, kabuli chana*) soaked, boiled and drained
1 tbsp oil
¾ cup finely chopped onions
¼ cup finely chopped capsicum
2 tsp finely chopped garlic *(lehsun)*
⅓ cup grated carrot
⅓ grated *paneer* (cottage cheese)
1½ tbsp dry red chilli flakes
1½ tsp *chaat masala*
½ tsp chilli powder
Salt to taste
2 tbsp finely chopped coriander *(dhania)*
¾ cup bread crumbs
½ cup plain flour *(maida)* dissolved in ¾ cup water for rolling
Oil for deep-frying

For the brown onions
16 onion rings
2 tbsp sugar

To be mixed into a curd spread
1 cup hung curds *(dahi)*, refer handy tip
1 tbsp chilled milk
1 tbsp fresh cream
A pinch of sugar
1½ tbsp chilli sauce
½ tsp mustard sauce
Salt to taste

To be mixed into an uncooked salsa
1 cup deseeded and finely chopped tomatoes
2 tbsp finely chopped capsicum
¼ cup finely chopped coriander *(dhania)*
1 tsp finely chopped green chillies
½ tsp cumin seeds *(jeera)* powder
½ tsp oregano
Salt to taste

Other ingredients
4 burger buns
4 tsp melted butter
4 lettuce leaves
4 cheese slices
1 tbsp dry red chilli flakes

Accompaniments
Onion Rings, page 39

For the *cutlets*
1. Heat the oil in a non- stick pan, add the onions, capsicum and garlic and sauté on a medium flame for 2 to 3 minutes.
2. Add the mixed beans, carrots and *paneer* and sauté on a medium flame for 2 to 3 minutes.
3. Add the chilli flakes, *chaat masala*, chilli powder and salt, mix well and cook on a medium flame for another 2 minutes.
4. Add the coriander and ¼ cup of bread crumbs and mix well.
5. Remove from the flame and mash it to a coarse mixture using a potato masher. Keep aside to cool.
6. Divide the mixture into 4 equal portions and shape each portion into a circle of 75 mm. (3") diameter and 1 cm thickness.
7. Dip each *cutlet* in the plain flour mixture and roll in the remaining bread crumbs till it is evenly coated from all the sides.
8. Heat the oil in a *kadhai* and deep-fry each *cutlet* till it turns golden brown in colour from both the sides. Drain on absorbent paper and keep aside.

For the brown onions
1. Heat a non-stick pan, add the onions and sugar and sauté on a high flame for 5 minutes or till the onions are golden brown in colour, while stirring occasionally.
2. Remove from the flame and keep aside.

How to proceed

1. Cut each burger bun horizontally into two. Apply ½ tsp of butter on the insides of each half of the burger bun and toast them lightly on a *tava* (griddle). Keep aside.
2. Place the lower half of a bun on a clean, dry surface with the buttered side facing up.
3. Place lettuce leaf and apply 2 tbsp of the curd spread and 2 tbsp of the salsa over it.
4. Place a *cutlet*, 1 slice of cheese and 4 brown onion rings and sprinkle a little chilli flakes over it.
5. Cover with an upper half of a bun with the buttered side facing down and press it lightly.
6. Repeat with the remaining ingredients to make 3 more burgers.
   Serve immediately with Onion Rings.

Handy tip : 2 cups of curds when tied in a muslin cloth and hanged for at least ½ hour gives approx. 1 cup of hung curds.

Broccoli
Burger

A burger with an exotic feel, this one can be made without much thought as broccoli is easily available in markets these days. The real flavour of this burger lies in cooking the broccoli to perfection, as over cooking or under-cooking will ruin the aroma, appearance and true flavour of the vegetable. Parsley, olives and mustard paste lend a variety of intriguing flavours to the otherwise bland mayonnaise making the spread quite tantalising. Serve the Brocolli Burger with an interesting accompaniment such as Dill Potatoes and Carrots, to make a perfect party treat.

PREPARATION TIME: 25 MINUTES.
COOKING TIME: 20 MINUTES.
MAKES 4 BURGERS.

For the *cutlets*
2 cups finely chopped broccoli
2 tsp oil
1 cup finely chopped onions
4 tsp finely chopped garlic (*lehsun*)
2½ tbsp finely chopped green chillies
1 cup boiled, peeled and mashed potatoes
4 tbsp cornflour
Salt to taste
½ cup plain flour (*maida*) dissolved in ¾ cup water for rolling
Bread crumbs for rolling
Oil for deep-frying

To be mixed into parsley mayonnaise spread
½ cup mayonnaise
½ cup finely chopped parsley
1 tbsp chopped green olives
1 tsp mustard paste

Other ingredients
4 burger buns
4 tsp melted butter
½ cup mayonnaise
4 lettuce leaves
4 cheese slices
8 cucumber slices
4 tomato slices
4 onion slices
Salt and freshly ground pepper to taste

Accompaniments
Dill Potatoes and Carrots, page 40

For the *cutlets*
1. Heat the oil in a broad non-stick pan, add the onions, garlic and green chillies and sauté on a medium flame till the onions turn translucent.
2. Add the broccoli and sauté on a medium flame for another 4 to 5 minutes or till the broccoli is almost cooked.
3. Remove from the flame, add the potatoes, cornflour and salt and mix well.
4. Divide it into 4 equal portions and shape each portion into a circle of 75 mm. (3") diameter and 1 cm thickness.
5. Dip each *cutlet* in the plain flour mixture and roll it the bread crumbs till it is evenly coated from all the sides.
6. Heat the oil in a *kadhai* and deep-fry each *cutlet* till it turns golden brown in colour from both the sides. Drain on absorbent paper and keep aside.

How to proceed
1. Cut each burger bun horizontally into two. Apply ½ tsp of butter on the insides of each half of the burger bun and toast them lightly on a *tava* (griddle). Keep aside.
2. Apply 1 tbsp of the mayonnaise on the buttered side of all the bun halves.
3. Place the lower half of a bun on a clean, dry surface with the buttered-mayonnaise side facing up.
4. Place 1 lettuce leaf, a *cutlet* and 1 cheese slice over it.
5. Apply 2 tbsp of the parsley mayonnaise spread and place 2 cucumber slices, 1 tomato slice and 1 onion slice over it.
6. Finally sprinkle a little salt and pepper over it.
7. Cover with an upper half of a bun with the buttered-mayonnaise side facing down and press it lightly.
8. Repeat with the remaining ingredients to make 3 more burgers.
   Serve immediately with Dill Potatoes and Carrots.

Falafel
Burger

*E*xplore the delights of international cuisines with this wonderful Lebanese burger recipe that features kabuli chana cutlet, and is served with Tabbouleh. The bread slice, although used only meagrely is very important to bind the cutlet, while the garlic and mint leaves make these cutlets very flavourful. What is more, the Falafel Burger features a tasty and colourful vegetable spread, which adds crunch to every mouthful.

PREPARATION TIME: 20 MINUTES.
COOKING TIME: 10 MINUTES.
MAKES 4 BURGERS.
SOAKING TIME: OVERNIGHT.

For the *cutlets*
1½ cups *kabuli chana* (chick peas)
½ cup roughly chopped onions
1½ tbsp chopped garlic (*lehsun*)
½ cup chopped coriander (*dhania*)
2 tbsp roughly chopped green chillies
1 tsp lemon juice
3 tbsp chopped mint leaves (*phudina*)
1 bread slice
Salt to taste
½ cup plain flour (*maida*) dissolved in ¾ cup water for rolling
Bread crumbs for rolling
Oil for deep-frying

To be mixed into a vegetable spread
⅓ cup hung curds (*dahi*), refer handy tip
½ tsp finely chopped garlic (*lehsun*)
¼ cup capsicum, cut into juliennes
¼ cup shredded purple cabbage
¼ cup grated carrots
A pinch of sugar
Salt to taste

Other ingredients
4 burger buns
4 tsp melted butter
4 lettuce leaves
4 cheese slice
4 cucumber slices
4 tomato slices
4 onion slices
Salt and freshly ground pepper to taste

Accompaniments
Tabbouleh, page 41

For the *cutlets*
1. Soak the *kabuli chana* in enough water in a deep bowl overnight. Drain well.
2. Combine all the ingredients and blend in a mixer to a coarse mixture using 2 tbsp of water.
3. Transfer the mixture into a bowl, divide it into 4 equal portions and shape each portion into a circle of 75 mm. (3") diameter and 1 cm thickness.
4. Dip each *cutlet* in the plain flour mixture and roll in the bread crumbs till it is evenly coated from all the sides.
5. Heat the oil in a *kadhai* and deep-fry each *cutlet* till it turns golden brown in colour from both the sides. Drain on absorbent paper and keep aside.

How to proceed
1. Cut each burger bun horizontally into two. Apply ½ tsp of butter on the insides of each half of the burger bun and toast them lightly on a *tava* (griddle). Keep aside.
2. Place the lower half of a bun on a clean, dry surface with the buttered side facing up.
3. Place 1 lettuce leaf, 1 cheese slice, 1 cucumber slice, 1 tomato slice and 1 onion slice and sprinkle a little salt and pepper over it.
4. Place a *cutlet* and apply ¼th of the vegetable spread over it.
5. Cover with an upper half of a bun with the buttered side facing down and press it lightly.
6. Repeat with the remaining ingredients to make 3 more burgers.
   Serve immediately with Tabbouleh.

Handy tip : ¾ cup of curds when tied in a muslin cloth and hanged for at least ½ hour gives approx. ⅓ cup of hung curds.

Spicy Paneer Burger

*T*hink spicy and our Indian masalas are sure to spring up in your mind! Yes, this cutlet features a blend of common Indian spices, ensuring a top rating by our desi taste buds. The mint chutney used in this recipe uses a good lot of onions, resulting in a very unusual flavour. When teamed with mayonnaise, it gives the Spicy Paneer Burger a tantalising taste that will linger in your tongue for a long time. Another exceptional point in this recipe is that it requires a lot of bread crumbs for binding, since the paneer is cooked.

PREPARATION TIME: 25 MINUTES.
COOKING TIME: 20 MINUTES.
MAKES 4 BURGERS.

For the *cutlets*
1¼ cups grated *paneer* (cottage cheese)
½ cup curds *(dahi)*
1½ tsp chilli powder
¼ tsp turmeric powder *(haldi)*
¾ tsp ginger *(adrak)* paste
½ tsp garlic *(lehsun)* paste
1 tsp *besan (*Bengal gram flour*)*
¾ tsp *chaat masala*
½ tsp dried fenugreek leaves (*kasuri methi*)
¾ tsp *garam masala*
Salt to taste
1 tbsp oil
2 tbsp finely chopped onions
2 tbsp finely chopped capsicum
¾ cup bread crumbs
½ cup plain flour (*maida*) dissolved in ¾ cup water for rolling
Oil for deep-frying

For the mint *chutney* (makes approx ⅓ cup)
1 cup chopped mint leaves (*phudina*)
½ cup chopped coriander (*dhania*)
1 cup roughly chopped onions
1 tbsp lemon juice
½ tbsp sugar
2 green chillies, roughly chopped
½ tsp roughly chopped ginger (*adrak*)
Salt to taste

To be mixed for the minty-mayo spread
⅓ cup mint *chutney*, recipe above
½ cup mayonnaise

To be mixed into a salad
¼ cup capsicum, cut into juliennes
¼ cup shredded cabbage
¼ cup thinly sliced onions
¼ cup finely chopped spring onion greens
¼ cup carrot juliennes
1 tsp *chaat masala*

Other ingredients
4 burger buns
4 tsp melted butter
4 cheese slices
4 lettuce leaves

Accompaniments
Masala French Fries, page 42

For the *cutlets*
1. Combine the curds, chilli powder, turmeric powder, ginger paste, garlic paste, *besan*, *chaat masala*, dried fenugreek leaves, *garam masala* and salt in a bowl and mix well.
2. Add the *paneer*, mix well and keep aside to marinate for 15 minutes.
3. Heat the oil in a broad non-stick pan and add the onions, capsicum and a little salt and sauté on a medium flame for 2 minutes.
4. Add the marinated *paneer*, mix well and sauté on a high flame for a minute.
5. Mash the mixture using a potato masher and sauté the *paneer* on a medium flame for another 5 minutes.
6. Remove from the flame, add ¼ cup of bread crumbs and mix well. Keep aside to cool slightly.
7. Divide the mixture into 4 equal portions and shape each portion into a circle of 75 mm. (3") diameter and 1 cm thickness.
8. Dip each *cutlet* in the plain flour mixture and roll in the remaining bread crumbs till it is evenly coated from all the sides.
9. Heat the oil in a *kadhai* and deep-fry each *cutlet* till it turns golden brown in colour from both the sides. Drain on absorbent paper and keep aside.

For the mint *chutney*
Combine all the ingredients and blend in a mixer to a smooth paste using a little water if required.

How to proceed
1. Cut each burger bun horizontally into two. Apply ½ tsp of butter on the insides of each half of the burger bun and toast them lightly on a *tava* (griddle). Keep aside.
2. Apply 1 tbsp of the minty-mayo spread on the buttered side of all the bun halves.
3. Place the lower half of bun on a clean, dry surface with the buttered-spread side facing up.
4. Place a *cutlet* and 1 slice of cheese over it.
5. Spread 1 tbsp of salad and again 1 tbsp of the minty-mayo spread evenly over it.
6. Place 1 lettuce leaf and cover with an upper half of a bun with the buttered-spread side facing down and press it lightly.
7. Repeat with the remaining ingredients to make 3 more burgers.
   Serve immediately with Masala French Fries.

Handy Tip: To get crunchy salad, combine only the vegetables in a deep bowl and immerse them in cold water for atleast 15 minutes. Drain, add the *chaat masala* and mix well. Use as required.

Chinese
Burger

You would have heard of Chinese bhel, Chinese dosa, and so on… but definitely not a Chinese burger! This unique recipe is sure to be a huge hit with any audience. The spread makes use of Schezuan sauce, to give a tangy, spicy touch, and cabbage leaves are used instead of lettuce to enhance the Chinese feel. The salad used in the burger is a slight variant of Kung Phao Potatoes, and lends another unique point of view to this recipe. Serve it with a traditional Chinese salad – Khimchi, for a well-rounded Chinese offering.

PREPARATION TIME: 25 MINUTES.
COOKING TIME: 20 MINUTES.
MAKES 4 BURGERS.

For the *cutlets*
¼ cup finely chopped French beans
¼ cup finely chopped carrots
¼ cup finely chopped capsicum
¼ cup finely chopped spring onions (greens)
2 tbsp finely chopped spring onions (whites)
1 tbsp oil
½ tsp finely chopped garlic (*lehsun*)
2 tsp soya sauce
1 tsp chilli powder
1¼ cups boiled, peeled and mashed potatoes
Salt to taste
Bread crumbs for rolling
½ cup plain flour (*maida*) dissolved in ¾ cup water for rolling
Oil for deep-frying

For the salad
2 tbsp oil
½ cup finely chopped spring onions (with the greens)
1 cup boiled potatoes, peeled and cut into fingers
Salt to taste
1 tbsp finely chopped coriander (*dhania*)
¼ cup Schezuan sauce

To be mixed into a Schezuan Mayo spread
2 tbsp Schezuan sauce
½ cup mayonnaise

Other ingredients
4 burger buns
4 tsp melted butter
4 cabbage leaves or lettuce
4 yellow capsicum rings

Accompaniments
Khimchi, page 43

For the *cutlets*
1. Heat the oil in a broad non- stick pan, add the garlic and sauté on a medium flame for a few seconds.
2. Add the spring onion whites and greens and sauté on a medium flame for a minute.
3. Add the French beans, carrots and capsicum and cook on a medium flame for 3 to 4 minutes or till the vegetables are cooked, while stirring occasionally.
4. Add the soya sauce and chilli powder, mix well and cook on a medium flame for another minute.
5. Add the potatoes and salt, mix well and cook on a medium flame for 2 more minutes.
6. Remove from the flame and keep aside to cool.
7. Divide it into 4 equal portions and shape each portion into a circle of 75 mm. (3") diameter and 1 cm thickness.
8. Dip each *cutlet* in the plain flour mixture and roll it in bread crumbs till it is evenly coated from all the sides.
9. Heat the oil in a *kadhai* and deep-fry each *cutlet* till it turns golden brown in colour from both the sides. Drain on absorbent paper and keep aside.

For the salad
1. Heat the oil in a broad non-stick pan and add the spring onions and sauté on a medium flame for a minute.
2. Add the potatoes, salt, coriander and Schezuan sauce and sauté on a medium flame for another 2 minutes.
3. Remove from the flame, divide it into 4 equal portions and keep aside.

How to proceed
1. Cut each burger bun horizontally into two. Apply ½ tsp of butter on the insides of each half of the burger bun and toast them lightly on a *tava* (griddle). Keep aside.

2. Apply 1 tbsp of the Schezuan Mayo spread on the buttered side of all the bun halves.
3. Place the lower half of a bun on a clean, dry surface with the buttered-spread side facing up.
4. Place 1 cabbage leaf or lettuce, capsicum ring and a *cutlet* over it.
5. Spread a portion of the salad over it and cover an upper half of a bun with the buttered-spread side facing down and press it lightly.
6. Repeat with the remaining ingredients to make 3 more burgers.
   Serve immediately with *Khimchi*.

Batata Vada Burger

*T*he Batata Vada Burger can be thought of as a variant of Mumbai's famous vada pav, which is made using batata vada and pav bun. In this variant, the authentic vadas are stuffed inside burger buns with two types of chutneys drizzled over mayonnaise. The use of a traditional salad, lettuce leaves and cheese make this burger different from the regular vada pav. I suggest you add a bunch of onion rings while serving this burger to make it all the more inviting.

PREPARATION TIME: 25 MINUTES.
COOKING TIME: 15 MINUTES.
MAKES 4 BURGERS.

For the *batata vada*
2 cups boiled, peeled and mashed potatoes
1 tbsp oil
¾ tsp mustard seeds (*rai/ sarson*)
¼ tsp asafoetida (*hing*)
10 curry leaves (*kadi patta*)
1½ tbsp ginger-green chilli paste
½ tbsp garlic (*lehsun*) paste
½ tsp turmeric powder (*haldi*)
Salt to taste
Oil for deep-frying

To be mixed together into a batter for the *vada*
⅓ cup *besan* (Bengal gram flour)
A pinch of turmeric powder (*haldi*)
Salt to taste
A pinch soda-bi-scarb
¼ cup water

To be mixed into a salad
½ cup finely chopped onions
½ cup finely chopped cucumber
½ cup finely chopped tomatoes
2 tbsp finely chopped coriander (*dhania*)
1 tsp finely chopped green chillies
1½ tbsp crushed peanuts
2 tsp dry garlic (*lehsun*) chutney, refer handy tip
Salt to taste

Other ingredients
4 burger buns
4 tsp melted butter
8 tbsp *meetha chutney*, refer handy tip
8 tbsp *teekha chutney*, refer handy tip
4 lettuce leaves
4 cheese slices

Accompaniments
Minty Onion Rings, page 44
Meetha chutney, page 29
Teekha chutney, page 29

For the *batata vada*
1. Heat the oil in a *kadhai* and add the mustard seeds.
2. When the seeds crackle, add the asafoetida and curry leaves and sauté on a medium flame for a few seconds.
3. Add the ginger-green chilli paste and garlic paste and sauté on a medium flame for another minute.
4. Add the potatoes, turmeric powder and salt, mix well and cook on a medium flame for more 2 minutes, while stirring continuously. Remove from the flame and keep aside to cool.
5. Divide it into 4 equal portions and shape each portion into a circle of 75 mm. (3") diameter and 1 cm thickness.
6. Heat the oil in a *kadhai,* dip each *vada* in the prepared batter and deep-fry till it turns golden brown in colour from all the sides. Drain on absorbent paper and keep aside.

How to proceed
1. Cut each burger bun horizontally into two. Apply ½ tsp of butter on the insides of each half of the burger bun and toast them lightly on a *tava* (griddle). Keep aside.
2. Spread 1 tbsp of *meetha chutney* and1 tbsp of *theeka chutney* on the buttered-*chutney* side of all the bun halves.
3. Place the lower half of a bun on a clean, dry surface with the buttered-*chutney* side facing up.
4. Place 1 lettuce leaf, 1 slice of cheese and a vada and spread 2 tbsp of the salad evenly over it.
5. Cover with an upper half of a bun with the buttered-*chutney* side facing down and press it lightly.
6. Repeat with the remaining ingredients to make 3 more burgers.
   Serve immediately with Minty Onion Rings, *meetha chutney* and *theeka chutney*.

Handy tips :

To make dry garlic *chutney* **(approx. ½ cup),** combine ⅓ cup peeled and roasted garlic, ¼ cup grated and roasted dried coconut, 2 tbsp chilli powder, 1 tsp coriander seeds powder, 1 tsp oil and salt to taste and blend in a mixer to a dry powder. Use as required.

To make *meetha chutney* **(approx. 1 cup),** combine ⅓ cup deseeded dates, 1 tbsp deseeded tamarind and 2 to 3 tbsp grated jaggery along with ⅓ cup of water and pressure cook for 2 whistles. Cool, blend in a mixer to a paste and strain using a sieve. Add ¼ tsp chilli powder, ⅛ tsp cumin seeds (*jeera*) powder and salt to taste and mix well. Use as required.

To make *teekha chutney* **(approx. 1 cup),** combine 1 cup roughly chopped coriander, 4 to 5 green chillies, 2 tsp chopped ginger, 1 tsp lemon juice and salt to taste along with ¼ cup of water and blend in a mixer to a smooth paste. Use as required.

Corn and Chick Pea Burger

*T*he cutlet in this burger features an unusual duo - sweet corn and kabuli chana. Another unique aspect of this cutlet is that it uses a combination of oats and bread slices as a binding agent. Fresh coriander combined with a bouquet of dried herbs along with lemon juice energises the refreshing green mayonnaise spread. Top it with scrumptious veggies like lettuce, cucumber, onions and tomatoes and serve with Spicy Potato Wedges, for a filling and delicious meal.

PREPARATION TIME: 15 MINUTES.
COOKING TIME: 15 MINUTES.
MAKES 4 BURGERS.

For the *cutlets*
1 cup boiled sweet corn kernels (*makai ke dane*)
1 cup soaked and cooked *kabuli chana* (chick peas)
1 tbsp oil
¼ cup chopped onions
1 bread slice, crumbled
2 tbsp *besan* (Bengal gram flour)
¼ cup quick cooking rolled oats
2 tsp chilli powder
Salt and freshly ground pepper to taste
½ cup plain flour (*maida*) dissolved in ¾ cup water for rolling
Bread crumbs for rolling
Oil for deep-frying

For the green mayonnaise spread
½ cup roughly chopped coriander (*dhania*)
1 tsp roughly chopped green chillies
1 tbsp roughly chopped onions
1 tsp lemon juice
½ cup mayonnaise
1 tsp dried mixed herbs

Other ingredients
4 burger buns
4 tsp melted butter
4 lettuce leaves
8 onion slices
8 tomato slices
12 cucumber slices
Salt and freshly ground pepper to taste

Accompaniments
Spicy Potato Wedges, page 45

For the *cutlets*
1. Heat the oil in a non-stick pan and add the onions and sweet corn and sauté on a medium flame for a minute.
2. Add the *kabuli chana*, bread, *besan*, oats, chilli powder, salt and pepper, mix well and sauté on a medium flame for 2 to 3 minutes. Keep aside to cool.
3. Add 2 tbsp of water and blend in a mixer to a coarse mixture.
4. Transfer the mixture into a bowl, divide it into 4 equal portions and shape each portion into a circle of 75 mm. (3") diameter and 1 cm thickness.
5. Dip each *cutlet* in the plain flour mixture and roll in the bread crumbs till it is evenly coated from all the sides.
6. Heat the oil in a *kadhai* and deep-fry each *cutlet* till it turns golden brown in colour from both the sides. Drain on absorbent paper and keep aside.

For the green mayonnaise
1. Combine the coriander, green chillies, onions and lemon juice and blend in a mixer to a coarse paste using ½ tbsp of water.
2. Transfer the paste into a deep bowl, add the mayonnaise and mixed herbs and mix well.
3. Keep refrigerated for at least an hour.

How to proceed
1. Cut each burger bun horizontally into two. Apply ½ tsp of butter on the insides of each half of the burger bun and toast them lightly on a *tava* (griddle). Keep aside.
2. Apply 1½ tbsp of the green mayonnaise spread on the buttered side of all the bun halves.
3. Place the lower half of a bun on a clean, dry surface with the buttered-spread side facing up.

4. Place 1 lettuce leaf, 2 onion slices, 2 tomato slices and 3 cucumber slices and sprinkle a little salt and pepper over it.
5. Place a *cutlet* and cover with an upper half of a bun with the buttered–spread side facing down and press it lightly.
6. Repeat with the remaining ingredients to make 3 more burgers.
   Serve immediately with Spicy Potato Wedges.

Top **10** Tips
to Yummy
Accompaniments

1. When making accompaniments it is very important to cut the vegetables of even shape and size so that they cook uniformly and also look good.

2. Pre-preps can be done in advance for all the recipes, but make the dish as close as to the serving time as possible.

3. All accompaniments are deep fried on a high or medium flame and never on slow flame. Follow it the procedure.

4. When adding *masalas* and spices to recipes like French fries and onion rings, make sure you add it immediately after deep frying and toss well.

5. After deep frying, always drain on absorbent paper to remove the excess oil.

Accompaniments

6 To make French fries use the variety of potatoes called French fries potatoes or Talegaon potatoes.

7 To save time, use ready-made French fries and potato wedges and follow the same procedure.

8 If the recipe calls for baking, grease the baking tray well to avoid the vegetables sticking to the tray.

9 When placing potatoes or chips on a baking tray, space them equally to ensure uniform cooking.

10 Be innovative by giving different shapes to vegetables like potatoes, carrots and cabbage.

Spicy Cheese and Herb Potato Wedges

*A*n accompaniment is very important for a burger, as it makes the meal more complete and also greatly enhances the temptation factor! A peppy plateful of Spicy Cheese and Herb Potato Wedges does this duty very, very well. A unique, well-chosen combination of herbs and spices makes these potato wedges very special, while garlic enhances its flavour and aroma. Bite in!

PREPARATION TIME: 10 MINUTES.
COOKING TIME: NIL.
SERVES 4.
BAKING TEMPERATURE: 200°C (400°F).
BAKING TIME: 35 TO 40 MINUTES.

2 cups potatoes, parboiled and cut into wedges (with the skin)
2 tbsp melted butter
1 tsp olive oil or oil
1 tsp grated garlic (*lehsun*)
4 tbsp grated cheese

For the spice mix
1 tbsp chilli powder
4 black peppercorns (*kalimirch*)
2 tsp dried basil
¼ tsp dried thyme
¼ tsp split mustard seeds (*rai na kuria*)
1 clove (*laung / lavang*)
1 tbsp salt

For the spice mix
1. Combine all the ingredients and blend in a mixer to a smooth powder.
2. Sieve the powder and keep aside.

How to proceed
1. Combine the potatoes, melted butter, olive oil, garlic and spice mix in a bowl and toss gently till the mixture coats the potatoes evenly.
2. Arrange the potatoes equally spaced on a greased baking tray and bake in a pre-heated oven at 200°C (400°F) for 25 to 30 minutes or till the potatoes are cooked. Turn over the potato wedges once in between after 10 to 12 minutes.
3. Sprinkle the cheese on top and again bake for another 3 to 4 minutes.
Serve immediately.

French
Fries

*F*rench Fries and burgers seem to have tied the knot! It is hard to think of burgers without some form of crispy accompaniment, but of these, the common French fries are the most tried-and-tested and safe combo for any type of burger. To enhance the visual appeal, cut the potatoes into fingers of uniform sizes. This also ensures uniform cooking. Let me also share a sure-shot tip with you – parboiling the potatoes before deep-frying results in the crunchiest French fries ever.

PREPARATION TIME: 10 MINUTES.
COOKING TIME: 20 MINUTES.
SERVES 4.

2 cups potatoes, peeled and cut into fingers
Salt and freshly ground pepper to taste
Oil for deep-frying

1. Boil a vesselful of water with a little salt. Add the potato fingers and parboil them for 5 to 7 minutes. Drain and keep aside.
2. Heat the oil in a *kadhai* and deep-fry a few potato fingers at a time on a medium flame till they turn crisp and golden brown in colour from all the sides.
3. Drain on absorbent paper, sprinkle salt and pepper on top and toss gently.
   Serve immediately.

Handy Tip : For really crisp French fries, use the variety of potatoes with a higher starch content popularly known as French Fries Potatoes/chips potatoes. In Maharashtra, they are called Talegaon potatoes.

Fried Mozzarella Sticks

For the batter
½ cup plain flour (*maida*)
¼ cup cornflour
½ tsp dried oregano
½ tsp dry red chilli flakes
Salt to taste

Other ingredients
250 gms mozzarella cheese
½ cup bread crumbs
Oil for deep-frying

*T*his crunchy accompaniment is cheese, cheese and cheese all the way through, so nothing can please cheese-lovers more! A simple flavouring of oregano and chilli flakes ensures that the overall effect is very pleasing. Fried Mozzarella Sticks can also be served as a party starter. Just keep a few things in mind when making it though… The oil should be very hot and the sticks should be deep-fried over a high flame. Also, you can double-coat the sticks with the batter and the crumbs so that the cheese does not ooze out of the covering.

PREPARATION TIME: 5 MINUTES.
COOKING TIME: 15 MINUTES.
MAKES 10 STICKS.

For the batter
Combine all the ingredients along with ½ cup of water in a bowl and mix well to make a thick batter. Keep aside.

How to proceed
1. Cut the mozzarella cheese into 10 long sticks of 75 mm. (3") x 25 mm. (1") with 1 cm. thickness.
2. Dip each cheese stick into the batter so that it is evenly coated on all the sides.
3. Roll each cheese stick in bread crumbs till it is evenly coated from all the sides.
4. Heat the oil in a *kadhai* and deep-fry 2 to 3 cheese sticks at a time on a high flame till they turn golden brown in colour from all the sides. Serve immediately.

Handy tip : While deep-frying, do not turn the sticks too many times as they might break and the cheese might ooze out.

Chilli Garlic Fries

An exotic accompaniment that can add zing even to the plainest of burgers, it is the smart use of melted butter and chopped garlic that sets the Chilli Garlic Fries apart from regular French fries. Sprinkle the chilli powder and butter-garlic mixture on the fries immediately after deep-frying and toss it well so that it coats the fries well from all sides. And... get ready for a real feast!

PREPARATION TIME: 10 MINUTES.
COOKING TIME: 15 MINUTES.
SERVES 4.

2 cups potatoes, peeled and cut into fingers
Salt to taste
1 tbsp butter
1½ tbsp finely chopped garlic (*lehsun*)
Oil for deep-frying
½ tsp chilli powder

1. Boil a vesselful of water with a little salt. Add the potato fingers and parboil them for 5 to 7 minutes. Drain and keep aside.
2. Heat the butter in a small *kadhai,* add the garlic and sauté for 30 seconds. Keep aside.
3. Heat the oil in a *kadhai,* and deep-fry a few potato fingers at a time on a medium flame till they turn crisp and golden brown in colour from all the sides. Drain on absorbent paper.
4. Pour the butter-garlic mixture and sprinkle the chilli powder on top and toss gently.
   Serve immediately.

Handy Tip: For really crisp French Fries, use the variety of potatoes with a higher starch content popularly known as French Fries Potatoes/chips potatoes. In Maharashtra, they are called Talegaon potatoes.

Cheesy Potato Chips

A quick fix accompaniment that you can use to spice up a simple layout of burgers and smoothies! Cheesy Potato Chips can be easily made using ready-made chips. Any variety of chips would do, but plain salted ones will suit the requirements better than flavoured ones. Do not over-bake as the chips might give a burnt taste and the cheese will become dry.

PREPARATION TIME: A FEW MINUTES.
COOKING TIME: NIL.
SERVES 4.
BAKING TEMPERATURE: 200°C (400°F).
BAKING TIME: 15 MINUTES.

2 cups readymade salted potato wafers
½ cup grated cheese
1 tsp chilli powder

1. Spread the potato wafers on a broad baking dish.
2. Sprinkle the cheese and chilli powder evenly over the wafers and bake in a pre-heated oven at 200°C (400°F) for 10 minutes. Serve immediately.

Onion
Rings

*A*lthough liked by people of all age groups, Onion Rings tops the charts as far as kids are concerned! The buttermilk added to the batter is a highlight of this recipe as it lends a unique flavour to the onion rings. Similarly, soda bi-carb is also essential to make the rings nice and fluffy. Toss the freshly-fried rings in chaat masala and watch with satisfaction as your children empty the plate in a jiffy!

PREPARATION TIME: 5 MINUTES.
COOKING TIME: 15 MINUTES.
SERVES 4.

20 onion rings
¾ cup plain flour (*maida*)
½ tsp cornflour
¾ cup buttermilk, refer handy tip
¼ tsp freshly ground pepper powder
A pinch of soda-bi-carb
Salt to taste
Oil for deep-frying
½ tsp *chaat masala*

1. Combine the plain flour, cornflour, buttermilk, pepper powder, soda-bi-carb and salt in a bowl and mix well to make a batter of pouring consistency.
2. Heat the oil in a *kadhai,* dip the onion rings in the batter a few at a time and deep-fry till they turn golden brown in colour from both the sides.
3. Drain on absorbent paper, sprinkle a little *chaat masala* over it and toss gently.
   Serve immediately.

Handy tip : To make ¾ cup of buttermilk, combine ¼ cup of fresh curds with ½ cup of water in a bowl, whisk well and use as per the recipe.

39

Dill Potatoes and Carrots

12 peeled baby potatoes
12 peeled and thickly sliced carrots
2 tbsp melted butter
1 tsp chopped dill leaves (*shepu / suva bhaji*)
Salt and freshly ground pepper to taste

*S*atays are a classic Oriental accompaniment featuring on most sizzler plates. Think different, and try them as an accompaniment to burgers. Although not a very commonly-used herb, dill graces this recipe with a very aesthetic flavour and lots of visual appeal as well!. Take care to add a little salt while boiling the vegetables to avoid any blandness, and enjoy Dill Potatoes and Carrots right off the barbeque!

1. Boil a vesselful of water with a little salt. Add the potatoes and carrots and parboil them for 5 to 7 minutes. Drain well and keep aside.
2. Combine the butter, dill leaves, salt and pepper in a bowl and mix well.
3. Add the potatoes and carrots and toss gently.
4. Thread 3 potatoes and 3 carrots alternatively on a skewer.
5. Repeat the step 4 to make 3 more skewers.
6. Grill the skewers over a charcoal or electric barbeque for 8 to 10 minutes or till they are lightly browned.
Serve immediately.

PREPARATION TIME: 10 MINUTES.
COOKING TIME: 15 TO 17 MINUTES.
SERVES 4.

Tabbouleh

Tabbouleh is a Lebanese salad that goes very well with the Falafel Burger, page 22. The Middle-Eastern influence governing both recipes ensures that the platter is picture-perfect. Parsley and mint are the key herbs featuring in this appealing salad, while broken wheat is another signature ingredient. Just take care not to overcook the broken wheat or else the dish might end up soggy.

PREPARATION TIME: 15 MINUTES.
COOKING TIME: 10 MINUTES.
SERVES 4.

½ cup broken wheat (*dalia*)
¼ cup finely chopped parsley
2 tbsp finely chopped mint leaves (*phudina*)
1 tbsp finely chopped spring onion greens
1 tbsp finely chopped spring onion whites
¼ cup finely chopped tomatoes
1 tbsp toasted sesame seeds (*til*)
1 tbsp lemon juice
1 tbsp olive oil
Salt to taste

1. Boil 2½ cups of water in a broad pan, add the broken wheat and cook on a medium flame for 10 minutes or till the broken wheat is cooked and all the water has been evaporated.
2. Transfer the broken wheat into a strainer and pour some cold water over it to cool it. Drain well.
3. Combine the broken wheat and all the vegetables in a deep bowl, toss well and refrigerate for at least an hour.
4. Just before serving, add the sesame seeds, lemon juice, olive oil and salt and toss well. Serve chilled.

Masala French Fries

The otherwise simple French fries takes on a very zingy feel when tossed with a horde of Indian masalas like chilli powder, cumin seeds powder, black salt and salt, making it a truly wonderful combination for burgers. Always deep-fry French fries on a medium flame as too slow a flame will make them soggy while a high flame will not cook them uniformly.

PREPARATION TIME: 10 MINUTES.
COOKING TIME: 15 MINUTES.
SERVES 4.

2 cups potatoes, peeled and cut into fingers
1 tsp chilli powder
1 tsp cumin seeds (*jeera*) powder
½ tsp black salt (*sanchal*)
Salt to taste
Oil for deep-frying

1. Boil a vesselful of water with a little salt. Add the potato fingers and parboil them for 5 to 7 minutes. Drain and keep aside.
2. Combine the chilli powder, cumin seeds powder, black salt and salt in a small bowl and keep the *masala* mixture aside.
3. Heat the oil in a *kadhai,* and deep-fry the potato fingers a few at a time on a medium flame till they turn crisp and golden brown in colour from all the sides.
4. Drain on absorbent paper, sprinkle the *masala* mixture on top and toss gently.
   Serve immediately.

Handy Tip: For really crisp French Fries, use the variety of potatoes with a higher starch content popularly known as French Fries Potatoes/chips potatoes. In Maharashtra, they are called Talegaon potatoes.

42

Khimchi

This crunchy, sweet and spicy preparation is the first dish that arrives when you dine at a Chinese restaurant. Khimchi would be a great accompaniment for the Chinese Burger, page 26, but you could also create trendy fusion combinations by serving it with other burgers from other cuisines. Serve it in crisp cabbage leaves to make it all the more appealing.

PREPARATION TIME: 5 MINUTES.
COOKING TIME: NIL.
MAKES 1 CUP.

1 cup cabbage, cut into 25 mm. (1") cubes
1 tsp chilli powder
1 tbsp powdered sugar
1 tbsp white vinegar
Salt to taste

1. Immerse the cabbage cubes in enough ice-cold water in a deep bowl for 1 hour.
2. Drain, add all the remaining ingredients and toss well.
   Serve immediately.

Minty Onion Rings

*M*inty Onion Rings can be whipped up in a jiffy with easily available ingredients. Use big-sized onions, and separate the rings carefully after slicing, to ensure that the chutney coats them evenly. Although easy, this recipe does taste quite different, because unlike the regular green chutney, this one uses more of mint leaves than coriander.

PREPARATION TIME: 10 MINUTES.
COOKING TIME: NIL.
SERVES 4.

1 cup onion rings

For the green *chutney*
1 cup roughly chopped mint leaves (*phudina*)
½ cup roughly chopped coriander (*dhania*)
1 tsp cumin seeds (*jeera*)
1 tbsp roughly chopped green chillies
1 tsp lemon juice
Salt to taste

For the green *chutney*
Combine all the ingredients and blend in a mixer to a smooth paste using a little water. Keep aside.

How to proceed
Combine the onion rings and green *chutney* in a bowl and mix gently.
Serve immediately.

Spicy
Potato
Wedges

*T*his scrumptious accompaniment of crispy
potato wedges with a generous sprinkling of
cheese is sure to double the appeal of any burger. It
takes a good lot of baking to ensure that the
unpeeled potato wedges are crisped to perfection,
but it is definitely worth the effort. What is more, a
bouquet of unusual herbs like rosemary and
oregano impart a rich and exotic feel that makes the
Spicy Potato Wedges all the more irresistible.

PREPARATION TIME: 10 MINUTES.
COOKING TIME: NIL.
SERVES 4.
BAKING TEMPERATURE: 200°C (400°F).
BAKING TIME: 30 TO 35 MINUTES.

2 cups potatoes, cut into wedges (with the skin)
2 tbsp melted butter
1 tbsp olive oil or oil
½ tbsp grated garlic (*lehsun*)
½ tsp dried oregano
½ tsp dried rosemary
½ tsp crushed pepper (*kalimirch*)
Salt to taste

1. Combine the potatoes, melted butter, olive oil,
   garlic, oregano, rosemary, pepper and salt in a
   bowl and toss till the mixture coats the
   potatoes evenly.
2. Arrange the potatoes equally spaced on a
   baking tray and bake in a pre-heated oven at
   200°C (400°F) for 25 to 30 minutes or until the
   potatoes are cooked, while turning over the
   potatoes once in between after 10 to 12
   minutes.
   Serve immediately.

Top 10 Tips to Luscious Smoothies

1. Deseed the fruits well before using them in the recipe.
2. Fruits like apples, chickoos and guava should always be peeled before using in smoothies.
3. Where mentioned in the recipe readymade fruit juices should be used, as some fresh juices might lend a bitter taste to the smoothie.
4. Whether using fruits, fruit juice, curds or milk, use them chilled.
5. Curds should always be fresh and thick.

Smoothies

6 Always pour the liquids first in the juicer followed by other ingredients.

7 Adjust the sugar and lemon juice for the recipes depending on the sweetness of the fruits.

8 Always serve smoothies immediately after blending.

9 Always serve in tall glasses.

10 Be creative to make your own garnishes with available ingredients.

Choco Chickoo Smoothie

*W*hat makes the Choco Chickoo Smoothie really different is the use of delicious chocolate ice-cream instead of vanilla ice-cream. The chocolate flavour combines beautifully with the chickoos.

PREPARATION TIME: 5 MINUTES.
COOKING TIME: NIL.
MAKES 2 BIG GLASSES.

1 cup chocolate ice-cream
1 cup chilled peeled, deseeded and roughly chopped chickoos
3 tbsp sugar
1 cup ice-cubes

For serving
4 tbsp crushed ice

For the garnish
2 chickoo wedges
2 mint sprigs

1. Combine the chocolate ice-cream, chickoos, sugar and ice-cubes and blend in a juicer till the mixture is smooth and frothy.
2. Place 2 tbsp of crushed ice into 2 individual glasses and pour equal quantities of the smoothie into each glass.
   Serve immediately garnished with a chickoo wedge and mint sprig on the rim of each glass.

Mango Apple Smoothie

Bookmark the Mango Apple Smoothie, and make sure you try it when the mango season is in full bloom. Milk balances the thickness of mangoes and apples to ensure the perfect smoothie consistency for your enjoyment.

PREPARATION TIME: 10 MINUTES.
COOKING TIME: NIL.
MAKES 2 BIG GLASSES.

1 cup chilled mango cubes
½ cup chilled and peeled apple cubes
¼ cup chilled full-fat milk
½ cup chilled fresh curds (*dahi*)
1½ tbsp sugar
1 cup ice-cubes

For the garnish
2 thin apple wedges

1. Combine the milk, ¼ cup of water, curds, mangoes, apples, sugar and ice-cubes and blend in a juicer till the mixture is smooth and frothy.
2. Pour equal quantities of the smoothie into 2 individual glasses.
   Serve immediately garnished with an apple wedge on the rim of each glass.

Pineapple Papaya Smoothie

*T*angy and crunchy pineapple and sweet and soft papaya might sound contrasting, but they are a perfect combination for a delicious smoothie! Adjust the sugar according to the sweetness of the fruits picked by you for the Pineapple Papaya Smoothie.

PREPARATION TIME: 10 MINUTES.
COOKING TIME: NIL.
MAKES 2 BIG GLASSES.

1 cup chilled and roughly chopped pineapple
⅓ cup chilled peeled, deseeded and roughly chopped papaya
¼ cup chilled fresh curds (*dahi*) mixed with ¼ cup chilled full-fat milk
3 tbsp sugar
½ cup ice-cubes

1. Combine the curds-milk mixture, pineapple, papaya, sugar and ice-cubes and blend in a juicer till the mixture is smooth and frothy.
2. Pour equal quantities of the smoothie into 2 individual glasses.
   Serve immediately.

Guava
Smoothie

The Guava Smoothie is a no-fuss drink that can be whipped up in a jiffy if you have guava juice and coconut milk ready in your fridge. Don't worry if coconut milk isn't available, simply replace it with equal amount of curds.

PREPARATION TIME: A FEW MINUTES.
COOKING TIME: NIL.
MAKES 2 BIG GLASSES.

1½ cups chilled guava juice, readily available
⅓ cup chilled coconut milk (*nariyal ka doodh*)
1½ cups vanilla ice-cream

For the topping
4 ice-cubes

1. Combine the guava juice, coconut milk and vanilla ice-cream and blend in a juicer till the mixture is smooth and frothy.
2. Pour equal quantities of the smoothie into 2 individual glasses.
   Serve immediately topped with 2 ice-cubes in each glass.

Handy tip : If coconut milk is unavailable, replace it with ⅓ cup of fresh curds and proceed as per the recipe.

Flax Seed
Smoothie

*T*he use of fibre-rich flax seeds and calcium and protein-rich soya milk lends a healthy angle to the Flax Seed Smoothie. At the same time, the lemon juice plays an indispensable role in enhancing the flavours of the scrumptious fruits used in this smoothie.

PREPARATION TIME: 5 MINUTES.
COOKING TIME: NIL.
MAKES 2 BIG GLASSES.

2 tbsp flax seeds (*alsi*)
1 cup vanilla flavoured soya milk
A few drops of lemon juice
1 cup chilled and roughly chopped strawberries
½ cup chilled and roughly chopped bananas
2 tbsp sugar

For the garnish
4 strawberries and 4 banana slices, threaded on 2 skewers

1. Combine the soya milk, lemon juice, strawberries, bananas, flax seeds and sugar and blend in a juicer till the mixture is smooth and frothy.
2. Pour equal quantities of the smoothie into 2 individual glasses.
   Serve immediately garnished with a strawberry and banana skewer in each glass.

Thai
Smoothie

*T*he Thai Smoothie is a drink with an Oriental touch. Chilled coconut milk gets a very flavourful boost with cardamom, our everyday Indian spice! When mangoes are in season, feel free to use them instead of canned mango pulp.

PREPARATION TIME: A FEW MINUTES.
COOKING TIME: NIL.
MAKES 2 BIG GLASSES.

½ cup chilled mango pulp
½ cup chilled thick coconut milk (*nariyal ka doodh*)
1 cup chilled fresh curds (*dahi*)
3 tbsp sugar
2 pinches cardamom (*elaichi*) powder

1. Combine the coconut milk, mango pulp, curds, sugar and cardamom powder and blend in a juicer till the mixture is smooth and frothy.
2. Pour equal quantities of the smoothie into 2 individual glasses.
   Serve immediately.

Peach Pineapple Smoothie

*T*he Peach Pineapple Smoothie draws its sweetness from honey rather than sugar, giving it a rich taste. Wheat germ along with curds helps achieve the perfect thickness for this smoothie. However, when wheat germ is not available, simply add some extra peaches.

PREPARATION TIME: 10 MINUTES.
COOKING TIME: NIL.
MAKES 2 BIG GLASSES.

1 cup chilled, peeled and roughly chopped peaches
1 cup chilled, roughly chopped pineapple
½ cup chilled fresh curds (*dahi*) mixed with ½ cup chilled full-fat milk
2 tbsp honey
2 tbsp wheat germ
½ cup ice-cubes

For the topping
4 tbsp crushed ice
4 peach juliennes

1. Combine the curds-milk mixture, honey, pineapple, peaches, wheat germ and ice-cubes and blend in a juicer till the mixture is smooth and frothy.
2. Pour equal quantities of the smoothie into 2 individual glasses.
   Serve immediately topped with 2 tbsp of crushed ice and garnished with 2 peach juliennes in each glass.

Grape Cranberry Smoothie

This tangy smoothie is sure to tingle your taste buds! Ensure you use good quality grapes that are ripe yet not soggy, so that your Grape Cranberry Smoothie results in the perfect mouth-feel, without leaving a sour aftertaste.

PREPARATION TIME: A FEW MINUTES.
COOKING TIME: NIL.
MAKES 2 BIG GLASSES.

1 cup chilled black grapes
¼ cup readymade chilled cranberry juice
¼ cup chilled fresh curds (*dahi*)
½ cup vanilla ice-cream
2 tbsp roughly chopped bananas
2 tbsp sugar

For the topping
4 tbsp crushed ice

1. Combine the cranberry juice, curds, vanilla ice-cream, black grapes, bananas and sugar and blend in a juicer till the mixture is smooth and frothy.
2. Pour equal quantities of the smoothie into 2 individual glasses.
   Serve immediately topped with 2 tbsp of crushed ice in each glass.

Melon
Smoothie

With the tanginess of orange and the creaminess of vanilla ice-cream, the not-so-popular muskmelon transforms into a delightful drink! Garnish the Melon Smoothie with a well-cut wedge of muskmelon to enhance its visual appeal.

PREPARATION TIME: 10 MINUTES.
COOKING TIME: NIL.
MAKES 2 BIG GLASSES.

1½ cups chilled, deseeded and roughly chopped muskmelon (*kharbooja*)
½ cup readymade chilled orange juice
4 tbsp chilled fresh curds (*dahi*)
½ cup vanilla ice-cream
2 tbsp sugar

For serving
2 muskmelon (*kharbooja*) wedges

1. Combine the orange juice, curds, vanilla ice-cream, muskmelon and sugar and blend in a juicer till the mixture is smooth and frothy.
2. Pour equal quantities of the smoothie into 2 individual glasses.
   Serve immediately garnished with a muskmelon wedge on the rim of each glass.

Pineapple and Orange Smoothie

*S*oothing muskmelon is a contrast to vivid pineapples, but with the balancing touch of oranges, the duo results in an irresistible Pineapple and Orange Smoothie! Use the readymade juices as suggested in the recipe, as fresh orange juice might be too sour and fresh pineapple juice too thick.

PREPARATION TIME: 10 MINUTES.
COOKING TIME: NIL.
MAKES 2 BIG GLASSES.

½ cup chilled and roughly chopped pineapple
¾ cup readymade chilled pineapple juice
¼ cup readymade chilled orange juice
½ cup vanilla ice-cream
½ cup chilled, deseeded and chopped muskmelon (*kharbooja*)
1 tbsp sugar

For serving
4 tbsp crushed ice

1. Combine the pineapple juice, orange juice, vanilla ice-cream, muskmelon, pineapple and sugar and blend in a juicer till the mixture is smooth and frothy.
2. Pour 2 tbsp of crushed ice into 2 individual glasses and pour equal quantities of the smoothie into each glass.
   Serve immediately.

Mango Banana Smoothie

*T*he Mango Banana Smoothie is a creamy, satiating smoothie – almost a meal in itself! Compared to other smoothies, this is very thick in consistency and hence milk and ice-cubes are added to liquidise it.

PREPARATION TIME: 10 MINUTES.
COOKING TIME: 20 SECONDS.
MAKES 2 BIG GLASSES.

1 cup chilled and roughly chopped mangoes
1 cup chilled and roughly chopped bananas
2 tbsp wheat germ
½ cup chilled fresh curds (*dahi*) mixed with ½ cup chilled full-fat milk
2 tbsp sugar
1 cup ice-cubes

For the garnish
6 mango cubes, threaded on 2 skewers

1. Spread the wheat germ in a microwave safe plate and microwave on HIGH for 20 seconds and keep aside.
2. Combine the curds-milk mixture, mangoes, bananas, wheat germ, sugar and ice-cubes and blend in a juicer till the mixture is smooth and frothy.
3. Pour equal quantities of the smoothie into 2 individual glasses.
   Serve immediately garnished with a mango skewer on the rim of each glass.

Kiwi
Smoothie

*T*he Kiwi Smoothie is sure to give your taste buds a wake-up call, as it imbibes the true flavours of the tangy kiwi fruit. This drink is to be consumed immediately as it might turn bitter in the course of time.

PREPARATION TIME: 10 MINUTES.
COOKING TIME: NIL.
MAKES 2 BIG GLASSES.

2 cups chilled, peeled and roughly chopped kiwi
4 tbsp chilled fresh curds (*dahi*)
1 cup vanilla ice-cream
4 tbsp sugar

For the garnish
2 kiwi slices

1. Combine the curds, vanilla ice-cream, kiwi and sugar and blend in a juicer till the mixture is smooth and frothy.
2. Pour equal quantities of the smoothie into 2 individual glasses.
   Serve immediately garnished with a kiwi slice on the rim of each glass.

Thandai
Smoothie

*T*he Thandai Smoothie is a fruit-less smoothie
with a rich and festive feel. Since the Thandai
*syrup is based mainly on spices, this smoothie is
generally liked more by adults than kids.*

PREPARATION TIME: A FEW MINUTES.
COOKING TIME: NIL.
MAKES 2 BIG GLASSES.

½ cup *Thandai* syrup
½ cup chilled fresh curds (*dahi*) mixed with ½ cup
chilled full-fat milk
4 tbsp vanilla ice-cream
½ cup ice-cubes

For the garnish
2 almonds (*badam*)

1. Combine the curds-milk mixture, *Thandai*
   syrup, vanilla ice-cream and ice-cubes and
   blend in a juicer till the mixture is smooth and
   frothy.
2. Pour equal quantities of the smoothie into 2
   individual glasses.
   Serve immediately garnished with an almond
   on the rim of each glass.

Orange and Strawberry Smoothie

A whopping hit with people of all age groups, fresh strawberries are at the centre-stage as far as this smoothie goes. However, when strawberries are not in season, you can use strawberry crush instead to prepare the Orange and Strawberry Smoothie.

PREPARATION TIME: 10 MINUTES.
COOKING TIME: NIL.
MAKES 2 BIG GLASSES.

1 cup chilled and roughly chopped strawberries
1 cup readymade chilled orange juice
¼ cup chilled fresh curds (*dahi*)
¾ cup vanilla ice-cream
2 tbsp sugar

For serving
4 tbsp crushed ice

1. Combine the orange juice, curds, vanilla ice-cream, strawberries and sugar and blend in a juicer till the mixture is smooth and frothy.
2. Place 2 tbsp of crushed ice into 2 individual glasses and pour equal quantities of the smoothie into each glass.
   Serve immediately.

Apple and Date Smoothie

*T*he Apple and Date Smoothie is very soothing to the palate as both apples and dates lend a very balanced taste without any overpowering flavours. The smoothie also imbibes the natural sweetness of dates, making it all the more pleasing.

PREPARATION TIME: 10 MINUTES.
COOKING TIME: NIL.
MAKES 2 BIG GLASSES.

2 cups chilled, peeled and roughly chopped apples
8 black dates, deseeded and chopped
½ cup chilled fresh curds (*dahi*) mixed with ½ cup chilled full-fat milk
4 tbsp sugar
½ cup ice-cubes

For the garnish
2 apple cubes

1. Combine the curds-milk mixture, apples, dates, sugar and ice-cubes and blend in a juicer till the mixture is smooth and frothy.
2. Pour equal quantities of the smoothie into 2 individual glasses.
   Serve immediately garnished with an apple cube on the rim of each glass.

Anjeer
Smoothie

*A*njeer Smoothie, as the name suggests, is a dry fruit based smoothie with dried figs as the key ingredient. As a novel idea, coarsely powdered sweet biscuits have been added to impart thickness to the smoothie, since there are no fruits in this recipe.

PREPARATION TIME: 5 MINUTES.
COOKING TIME: NIL.
MAKES 2 BIG GLASSES.

8 dried figs (*anjeer*), soaked overnight
1 cup chilled milk
1 cup vanilla ice-cream
8 almonds (*badam*), soaked overnight and de-skined
⅓ cup coarsely crushed sweet biscuits (Parle G)
4 tbsp sugar
1 cup ice- cubes

For the garnish
2 dried figs (*anjeer*), each threaded on a toothpick

1. Combine the milk, vanilla ice- cream, dried figs, almonds, biscuits, sugar and ice-cubes and blend in a juicer till the mixture is smooth and frothy.
2. Pour equal quantities of the smoothie into 2 individual glasses.
   Serve immediately garnished with a fig on the rim of each glass.

Papaya Melon Smoothie

*T*he specialty of smoothies is that the strangest of ingredients combine well to give great results! You might never have thought of combining papayas and muskmelons, but try the Papaya Melon Smoothie and you are sure to fall in love with this combination.

PREPARATION TIME: 10 MINUTES.
COOKING TIME: NIL.
MAKES 2 BIG GLASSES.

1 cup chilled, peeled, deseeded and roughly chopped papaya
½ cup chilled, deseeded and roughly chopped muskmelon (*kharbooja*)
¼ cup chilled fresh curds (*dahi*) mixed with ¼ cup chilled full-fat milk
1 tbsp sugar
5 ice-cubes

For the topping
4 tbsp crushed ice

1. Combine the curds-milk mixture, papaya, muskmelon, sugar and ice-cubes and blend in a juicer till the mixture is smooth and frothy.
2. Pour equal quantities of the smoothie into 2 individual glasses.
   Serve immediately topped with 2 tbsp of crushed ice in each glass.

Banoffee
Smoothie

*D*id we say Banoffee Smoothie? As you might have smartly guessed, the name comes from a combination of bananas and coffee. The success of this smoothie lies in getting the decoction right. So, follow the method exactly as mentioned, and forget yourself in this heavenly drink.

PREPARATION TIME: A FEW MINUTES.
COOKING TIME: 1 MINUTE.
MAKES 2 BIG GLASSES.

For the coffee decoction
2 tsp coffee
2 ice-cubes

Other ingredients
½ cup chilled and roughly chopped bananas
¼ cup coffee decoction, recipe above
½ cup chilled full-fat milk
½ cup chilled fresh curds (*dahi*)
½ cup vanilla ice-cream
¼ cup sugar

For the topping   **For the garnish**
2 tbsp crushed ice   2 chocolate fans

For the coffee decoction
1. Put 1 tbsp of water in a microwave safe bowl and microwave on HIGH for 30 seconds.
2. Add the coffee powder and microwave on HIGH for another 30 seconds.
3. Remove from the microwave, add the ice-cubes and allow it to cool.
   Keep aside.

How to proceed
1. Combine the milk, coffee decoction, curds, vanilla ice-cream, bananas and sugar and blend in a juicer till the mixture is smooth and frothy.
2. Pour equal quantities of the smoothie into 2 individual glasses.
   Serve immediately topped with 1 tbsp of crushed ice in each glass and garnished with a chocolate fan on the rim of each glass.

Handy tip : The coffee decoction is likely to overflow when being heated in the microwave, hence keep a continuous watch.

Mango
and
Orange
Smoothie

*T*he Mango Orange Smoothie is sweet, tangy and totally lovable. Oh! no, but the mango season comes just once a year! Not to worry, make the mango pulp in bulk and enjoy this smoothie throughout the year.

PREPARATION TIME: A FEW MINUTES.
COOKING TIME: NIL.
MAKES 2 BIG GLASSES.

¾ cup chilled mango pulp
½ cup readymade chilled orange juice
4 tbsp chilled fresh curds (*dahi*)
½ cup vanilla ice-cream
1½ tbsp sugar

For serving
4 tbsp crushed ice

1. Combine the orange juice, mango pulp, curds, vanilla ice-cream and sugar and blend in a juicer till the mixture is smooth and frothy.
2. Place 2 tbsp of crushed ice into 2 individual glasses and pour equal quantities of the smoothie into each glass.
   Serve immediately.

Tropical
Smoothie

*T*he Tropical Smoothie is a balanced combination of papaya and pineapple blended with ever popular vanilla ice-cream. The zing of pineapple compensates well for the blandness of papaya, resulting in a smoothie worth a fortune!

PREPARATION TIME: 10 MINUTES.
COOKING TIME: NIL.
MAKES 2 BIG GLASSES.

1 cup chilled, peeled, deseeded and roughly chopped papaya
¾ cup chilled, roughly chopped pineapple
3 tbsp chilled fresh curds (*dahi*)
¾ cup vanilla ice-cream
4 tbsp sugar

For serving
4 tbsp crushed ice

1. Combine the curds, vanilla ice-cream, papaya, pineapple and sugar and blend in a juicer till the mixture is smooth and frothy.
2. Place 2 tbsp of crushed ice into 2 individual glasses and pour equal quantities of the smoothie into each glass.
Serve immediately.

67

Pear and Pomegranate Smoothie

Two interesting fruits – pear and pomegranate, not very commonly used in smoothies, are combined with curds, milk and ice cubes to make the comforting pink-coloured Pear and Pomegranate Smoothie. Adjust the sugar content according to the tanginess of the pomegranate.

PREPARATION TIME: 10 MINUTES.
COOKING TIME: NIL.
MAKES 2 BIG GLASSES.

2 cups chilled, peeled and roughly chopped pear
½ cup chilled pomegranate
¼ cup chilled fresh curds (*dahi*) mixed with ¼ cup chilled full-fat milk
2 tbsp sugar
1 cup ice-cubes

For the topping
4 ice-cubes

1. Combine the curds-milk mixture, pear, pomegranate, sugar and ice-cubes and blend in a juicer till the mixture is smooth and frothy.
2. Pour equal quantities of the smoothie into 2 individual glasses.
   Serve immediately topped with 2 ice-cubes in each glass.

Apple
Smoothie

You can never go wrong with apples! You can confidently use apples in any smoothie, especially along with any fruit-based crush readily available in the market. Since both strawberry crush and vanilla ice-cream are used, there is no need to add any extra sugar for the Apple Smoothie.

PREPARATION TIME: 5 MINUTES.
COOKING TIME: NIL.
MAKES 2 BIG GLASSES.

1½ cups chilled, peeled and roughly chopped apples
5 tbsp strawberry crush
4 tbsp chilled fresh curds (*dahi*)
1 cup vanilla ice-cream

For the topping
4 tbsp crushed ice

1. Combine the curds, strawberry crush, vanilla ice-cream and apples and blend in a juicer till the mixture is smooth and frothy.
2. Pour equal quantities of the smoothie into 2 individual glasses.
   Serve immediately topped with 2 tbsp of crushed ice in each glass.

Banana
Oats
Smoothie

*T*he Banana Oats Smoothie, as you might have figured out already, is an intelligent choice for breakfast! The use of bananas, oats, flax seeds, curds and honey (instead of sugar) marks up the nutrition quotient of this recipe remarkably.

PREPARATION TIME: 5 MINUTES.
COOKING TIME: NIL.
MAKES 2 BIG GLASSES.

1 cup chilled and roughly chopped bananas
½ cup quick cooking rolled oats
1 cup chilled fresh curds (*dahi*)
2 tbsp honey
2 tbsp flax seeds (*alsi*)
½ cup ice-cubes

1. Combine the curds, honey, bananas, oats, flax seeds and ice-cubes and blend in a juicer till the mixture is smooth and frothy.
2. Pour equal quantities of the smoothie into 2 individual glasses.
   Serve immediately.

Blueberry and Apple Smoothie

Just like cheesecakes, mousses and other recipes made with blueberry crush, the Blueberry and Apple Smoothie is also a sure hit! Apples are used to make the smoothie thick without overpowering the sharp hints of blueberry.

PREPARATION TIME: 5 MINUTES.
COOKING TIME: NIL.
MAKES 2 BIG GLASSES.

6 tbsp blueberry crush
1 cup chilled, peeled and roughly chopped apples
½ cup chilled fresh curds (*dahi*) mixed with ½ cup of chilled full-fat milk
½ cup ice-cubes

For the garnish
4 thin apple wedges

1. Combine the curds-milk mixture, blueberry crush, apples and ice-cubes and blend in a juicer till the mixture is smooth and frothy.
2. Pour equal quantities of the smoothie into 2 individual glasses.
   Serve immediately garnished with 2 apple wedges on the rim of each glass.

TARLA DALAL COOKBOOKS

◆ Tarla Dalal's ◆
Snack & Drink Collection

SNACKS UNDER 10 MINUTES

KEBABS & TIKKIS

PARTY DRINKS

PANEER SNACKS

HEALTHY SNACKS

HEALTHY STARTERS

HEALTHY JUICES

Hurry get your copy today! | TARLA DALAL BOOKS ARE AVAILABLE AT ALL LEADING BOOK STORES ACROSS INDIA